Go Tell Aunt Rhody

Go Tell Aunt Rhody

Illustrated by Aliki

Macmillan Publishing Co., Inc.
New York

1   2   3   4   5   6   7   8   9   10

The pictures were painted in gouache.
The typeface is Garamond Old Style, composed photographically.

Library of Congress Cataloging in Publication Data
Main entry under title: Go tell Aunt Rhody.   1. Children's songs.
2. Folk-songs, American.   [1. Folk songs, American]   I. Aliki, illus.
M1998.G   784.4'973   74–681   ISBN   0–02–711920–3

For Jolly and Alfred and their little women,
Emily, Elizabeth, Kate and Nell

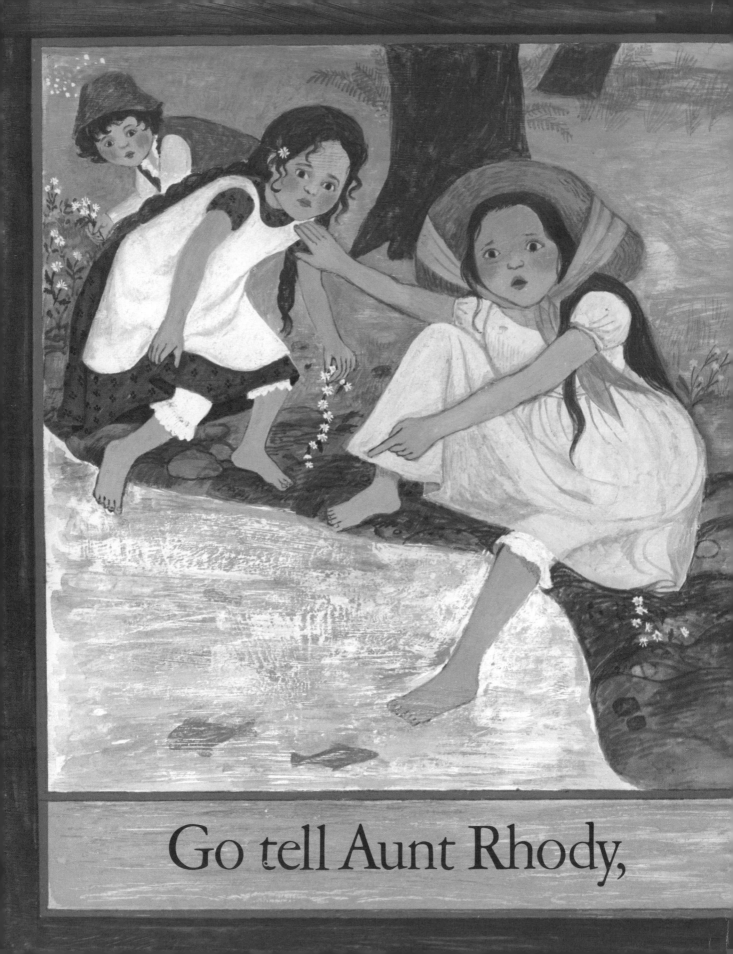

Go tell Aunt Rhody,

go tell Aunt Rhody,

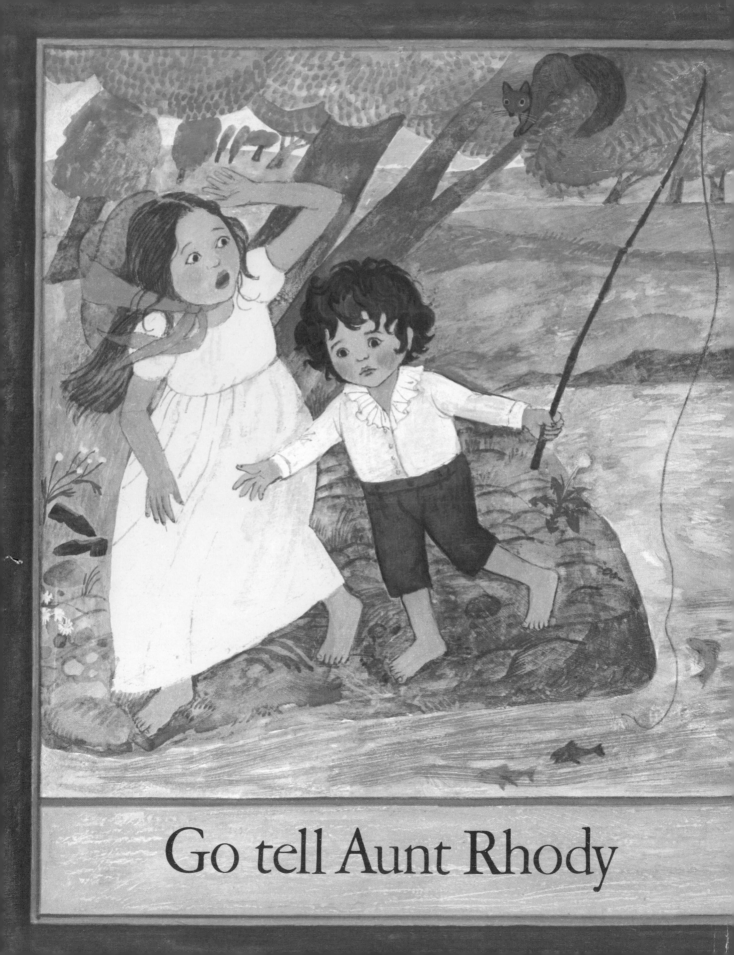

Go tell Aunt Rhody

the old gray goose is dead.

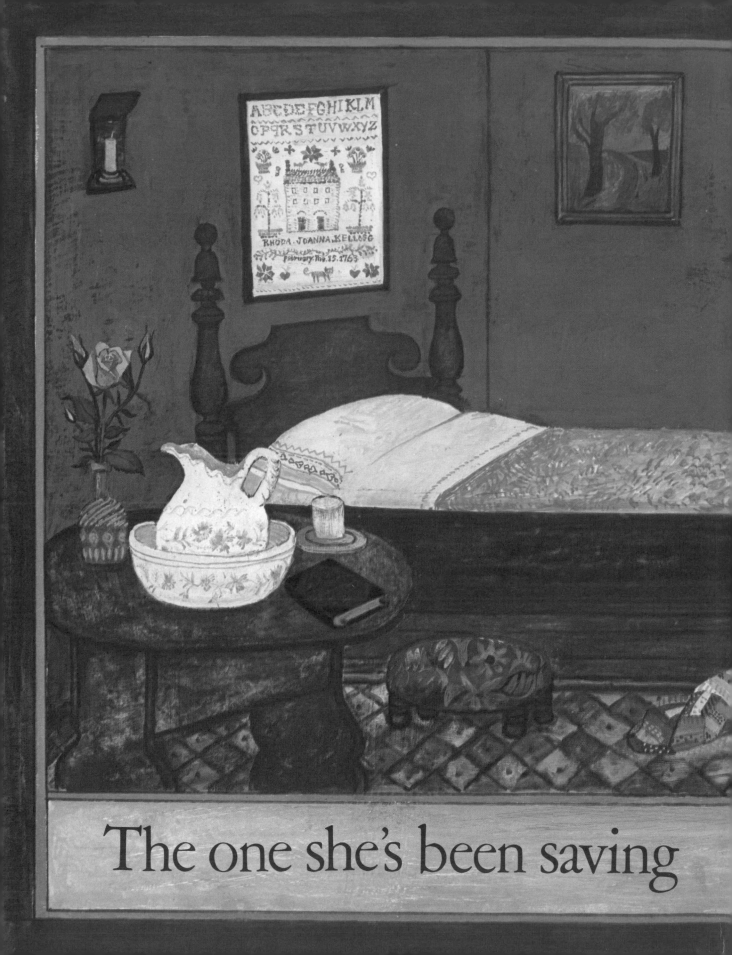

The one she's been saving

to make a feather bed.

The old gander's weeping

because his wife is dead.

The goslings are mourning

because their mother's dead.

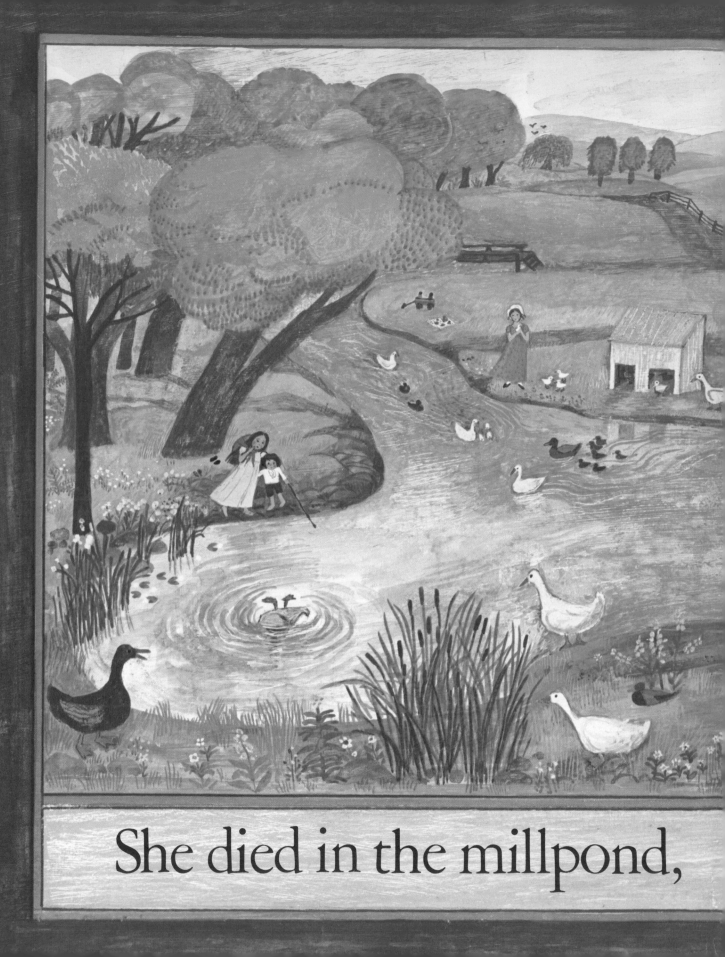

She died in the millpond,

standing on her head.

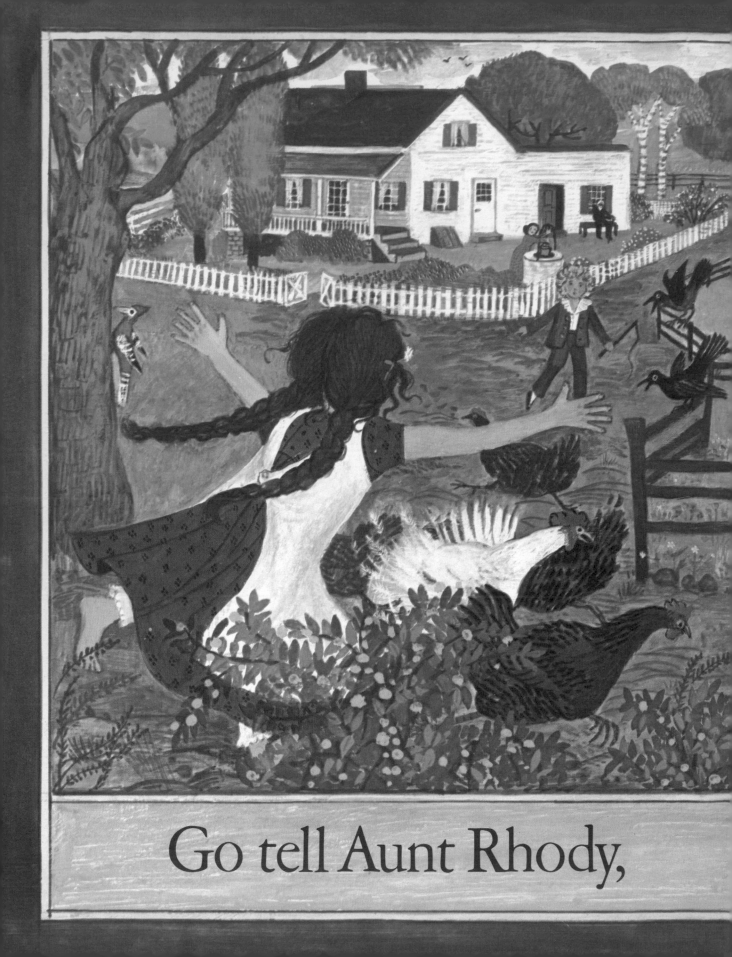

Go tell Aunt Rhody,

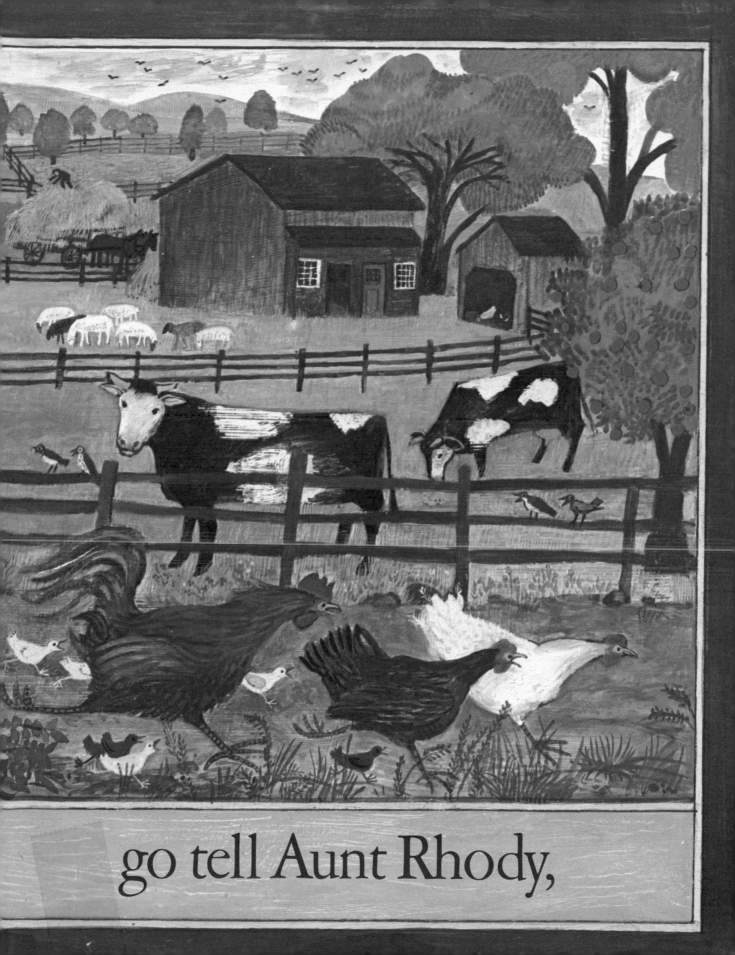

go tell Aunt Rhody,

Go tell Aunt Rhody

the old gray goose is dead.

Go Tell Aunt Rhody

F Major   C7

Traditional American Folk Song
Arranged by Gretchen Amussen

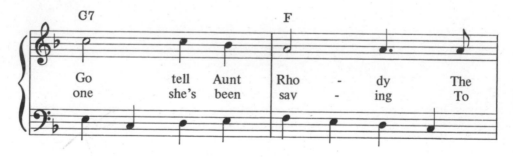

3. The old gander's weeping,
   The old gander's weeping,
   The old gander's weeping
   Because his wife is dead.

4. The goslings are mourning,
   The goslings are mourning,
   The goslings are mourning
   Because their mother's dead.

5. She died in the millpond,
   She died in the millpond,
   She died in the millpond,
   Standing on her head.

6. Go tell Aunt Rhody,
   Go tell Aunt Rhody,
   Go tell Aunt Rhody
   The old gray goose is dead.

"**Go Tell Aunt Rhody**" is a folk song that did not start out as a folk song. More than two hundred years ago a famous French writer and musician, Jean Jacques Rousseau, wrote an opera called *The Village Sooth-sayer.* The opera was performed in France for the king, Louis XV, and in England too. After many years, the opera was forgotten except for one melody in it. People played it on the piano, the harp and the guitar. Later the song reached the United States. Words were put to it, and one version was called "Go Tell Aunt Rhody." Over the years it has become a favorite lullaby.